Animal Attacks

MOOSE ATTACK

by Lisa Owings

BELLWETHER MEDIA · MINNEAPOLIS, MN

Are you ready to take it to the extreme?
Torque books thrust you into the action-
packed world of sports, vehicles, mystery,
and adventure. These books may include
dirt, smoke, fire, and dangerous stunts.
WARNING : read at your own risk.

Library of Congress Cataloging-in-Publication Data

Owings, Lisa.
 Moose attack / by Lisa Owings.
    p. cm. -- (Torque: animal attacks)
 Includes bibliographical references and index.
 Summary: "Engaging images illustrate true moose attack stories and accompany survival tips. The
combination of high-interest subject matter and light text is intended for students in grades 3 through 7"
--Provided by publisher.
 ISBN 978-1-60014-788-3 (hardcover : alk. paper)
 ISBN 978-1-60014-844-6 (paperback : alk. paper)
 1. Moose--Behavior--Juvenile literature. 2. Animal attacks--Juvenile literature. I. Title.
 QL737.U55O95 2013
 599.65'7153--dc23

                              2012011223

This edition first published in 2013 by Bellwether Media, Inc.

No part of this publication may be reproduced in whole or in part without written permission of the
publisher. For information regarding permission, write to Bellwether Media, Inc., Attention: Permissions
Department, 5357 Penn Avenue South, Minneapolis, MN 55419.

Text copyright © 2013 by Bellwether Media, Inc. TORQUE and associated logos are trademarks and/or
registered trademarks of Bellwether Media, Inc.

SCHOLASTIC, CHILDREN'S PRESS, and associated logos are trademarks and/or
registered trademarks of Scholastic Inc.

Printed in the United States of America, North Mankato, MN.

TABLE OF CONTENTS

Central Arkansas Library System
Oley Rooker Branch
Little Rock, Arkansas

Monstrous Moose

Did you know that moose are downright deadly? If not, you have never seen the **fury** of one of these 1,800-pound (820-kilogram) beasts. All moose have hooves sharp enough to split skulls. Males stab **rivals** with the bony spikes on their **antlers**. Females can stand their ground against grizzly bears and entire wolf packs to protect their young. You don't want to mess with a moose!

The Bull Moose

A male moose is called a bull moose. Bull moose have antlers that can grow up to 6 feet (1.8 meters) wide.

Hit and Run!

It was an unusually cold winter morning in Alaska. George Murphy and Dorothea Taylor were exercising their dogs near the local airport. The couple stayed warm in their truck while the dogs ran loose through the snow. Soon George got out to round up the dogs. As he approached them, he saw a huge moose running toward him. With nowhere else to hide, he dove into a snowbank.

Mortal Enemies

Moose and wolves are natural enemies. Dogs are so similar to wolves that moose are likely to attack them.

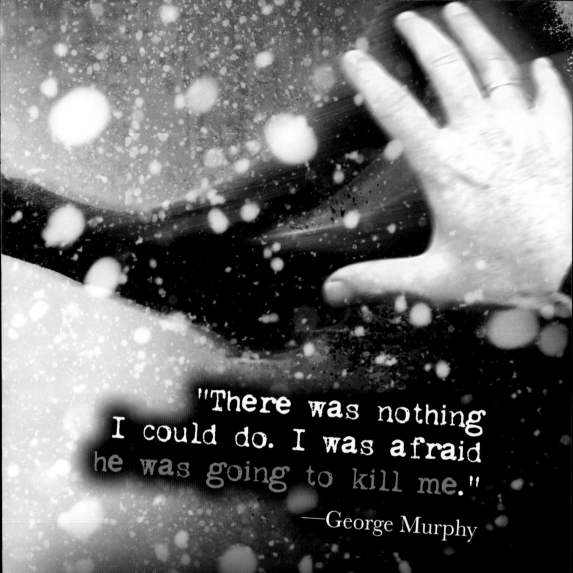

"There was nothing
I could do. I was afraid
he was going to kill me."

—George Murphy

George yelled for help as the moose **trampled**
him. Its sharp hooves split his head open and
crushed his ribs. Dorothea heard the dogs barking
in panic. She jumped out of the truck and saw the
moose. She thought it was attacking one of the
dogs. The 85-year-old rushed toward the animal
to drive it away. Then the moose **lunged** for her.

Dorothea ran to the truck and grabbed a shovel. She beat the moose with it, but the animal wouldn't move. Then she swung with all her strength. The moose backed off and was chased away by one of the dogs. Dorothea finally saw her husband bleeding in the snowbank. She ran for help. Thanks to her bravery, George made it to the hospital just in time.

Dorothea Taylor

"Slowly it turned and I hit it with everything I had."

—Dorothea Taylor

George Murphy

"That was a pretty hard thing for anyone to do, to walk up on a moose like that. Heck, all she had was a shovel."

—George Murphy

In Her Own Backyard

Caren della Cioppa was trimming bushes behind her Alaska home when she heard the rumble of hooves. Suddenly a moose **charged** out of the woods and knocked her down. Its hooves pounded into her chest. Her ribs and **collarbone** cracked under the animal's weight. After a final blow to her forehead, it was over. The moose was gone. Or so she thought.

"I remember thinking I might not make it through this."
—Caren della Cioppa

Mama Moose
Mother moose are extremely dangerous. They will attack anything they think might hurt their calves. The moose that attacked Caren had just given birth.

Caren needed help. She was having trouble breathing and could barely move. She felt for the cell phone in her pocket and dialed 911. When state troopers arrived minutes later, the moose reappeared. It leaped over Caren and thundered toward the troopers.

"The moose sounded like a freight train."
—Caren della Cioppa

Moose on the Loose

More people are injured by moose than bears each year in Alaska.

The troopers had to act fast. They pulled out their guns and fired at the angry moose. It dropped to the ground. Doctors at a nearby hospital treated Caren. The attack left her with several broken bones, a **dislocated** shoulder, and a bruised forehead. Her cell phone and the troopers had saved her from being trampled to death.

Caren della Cioppa

Caring for Calves

The Alaska Moose Federation took care of the moose's twin calves after the attack. They were released into the wild when they were old enough to live on their own.

Prevent a Moose Attack

Moose like their space. You can prevent an attack by keeping your distance. Back away if you find yourself too close to a moose. Do not bring dogs into moose **territory**. Their presence can **provoke** an attack.

Be extra careful in moose territory in fall and spring. Bull moose are most **aggressive** in the fall. This is when they compete for females. In spring, mother moose will attack to protect their young calves.

Danger Signs

You may be in trouble if you see a moose...

- walking toward you with its ears back
- stomping its feet
- swinging its head back and forth
- grunting

Survive a Moose Attack

A moose may charge if it feels **threatened**. Take cover behind a tree or large rock if you can. Run away quickly if there is no cover. Moose usually give up the chase before too long.

Curl into a ball and cover your head if you can't get away. This will help protect your body from trampling hooves. Do not move until you are sure the moose is gone. With a little luck, you will survive an encounter with the mighty moose.

21

Glossary

aggressive—violent and likely to attack

antlers—large, bony structures similar to horns on the heads of bull moose; moose antlers are wide and flat with spikes around the edges.

charged—rushed forward to attack

collarbone—the long, horizontal bone that makes up part of the shoulder; a person's collarbones sit below the neck and above the ribs.

dislocated—moved out of its usual place

fury—extreme anger, rage, or violence

lunged—moved forward suddenly

provoke—to bring on or stir to action

rivals—those who compete against each other; bull moose compete for females.

territory—the area of land where an animal lives, searches for food, and raises its young

threatened—likely to be in danger

trampled—stomped on heavily, causing severe injuries

To Learn More

AT THE LIBRARY

Gish, Melissa. *Moose*. Mankato, Minn.: Creative Education, 2010.

Goyette, Linda. *Northern Kids*. Victoria, BC: Brindle & Glass, 2010.

Winnick, Nick. *Moose*. New York, N.Y.: AV2, 2011.

ON THE WEB

Learning more about moose is as easy as 1, 2, 3.

1. Go to www.factsurfer.com.

2. Enter "moose" into the search box.

3. Click the "Surf" button and you will see a list of related Web sites.

With factsurfer.com, finding more information is just a click away.

Index

D1214766